I AM WHAT I AM

by
Roderick Cox and Tobias Lagemann

Cornelsen

I am what I am
Roderick Cox, Tobias Lagemann

Verlagsredaktion
Susanne Döpper

Umschlaggestaltung
Heike Börner, dia

Titelbilder
Pop-Eye, Berlin
Corel Library

Illustration
Kay Dixey, Linda Rogers Agency

Technische Umsetzung
Peter Richter

www.cornelsen.de

1. Auflage, 4. Druck 2011

Alle Drucke dieser Auflage sind inhaltlich unverändert und können im Unterricht nebeneinander verwendet werden.

Druck: Drogowiec-PL Spolka z o. o., Kielce

ISBN 978-3-464-34392-0

Inhalt gedruckt auf säurefreiem Papier aus nachhaltiger Forstwirtschaft.

CONTENTS

CHAPTER ONE

Luke Layton was standing on the street corner. On the other side of the street was the house that Tracy lived in. Luke looked up at her window. Will she see me? Tracy was the nicest girl in Year 10. No, Tracy was the nicest girl in the whole world. Tracy's face appeared at the window. Tracy smiled at Luke. Luke was happy.

RRRRINGGG!

Luke looked up at Tracy's window. Everything was black. Where was Tracy?

RRRRINGGG!

"Tracy," thought Luke, "where are you?"

Luke looked around. "Oh no," he thought. It was only a dream about Tracy – again.

RRINNN …

Luke switched the alarm clock off. "Only a dream," he thought. "The same dream – again!" He couldn't get Tracy out of his head.

"Luke," the boy heard his father's voice, "get up! Come on. Hurry up!"

Luke looked at the clock. It was almost 8 o'clock. His dad was right. He had to get up. The bus to school went in 40 minutes.

Luke got up. With tired eyes, he opened the door to his room. He could hear his dad making breakfast in the kitchen.

"Hurry up, Luke," his father shouted.

Luke went to the bathroom. Then he put his jeans on and a clean shirt. He had to look good for Tracy. Tracy was a really good-looking girl. All the boys in Luke's class talked about Tracy.

"Hurry up!"

Luke hurried up. It was time for breakfast.

"Good morning, Dad," Luke said to his father.

"Hi, son."

"Oh, *Krispie Pops*. Great!"

"For my favourite son his favourite breakfast," his dad said.

"You only have one son," said Luke.

"That's why you're my favourite son. I love you."

"Adults!" thought Luke and shook his head. Adults always say things you don't understand. "I never want to be an adult," thought Luke. And then he thought, "I love Tracy."

"What's the matter with you?" asked Luke's dad.

"Nothing," answered Luke.

"I know something is the matter, son!"

"No, no, Dad!" Luke looked at his plate.

"I'm always there for you, boy."

"I know."

"Tell me what's the matter."

Luke shook his head. "Nothing, Dad."

"Are you still enjoying your music?" his dad asked.

Luke smiled. "I am what I am."

"A musician!" his dad laughed.

"Yes, a musician," laughed Luke.

"You are you," said Luke's dad.

"I am what I am."

Luke wanted to be a musician. In his free time he wrote songs – rap songs. Luke rapped about the things that were important to him. Many songs were about music. Luke rapped about his friends, too. And of course he rapped about love. Love was such a beautiful thing. Luke only sang about beautiful things.

He didn't like gangsta rap. He wasn't a bad boy. He was one of the good boys. And Luke wanted to be a good musician.

"I'm proud of you," Luke's dad said. He knew what his son rapped about. "And you can always talk to me," he said.

"OK, Dad, I know."

"Promise you'll tell me about your problems."

"Of course, Dad," Luke said.

Luke felt bad. He wanted to tell his dad everything, but what did his dad know about love? Luke's parents were divorced. Luke remembered the time. It was five years ago now. Were his parents divorced because of him? He was fat and his mother was fat. But his father was slim. Luke wanted to be like his father.

Didn't Luke's dad like fat children? And didn't he like fat women? Luke wasn't really fat. He just wasn't slim. Luke had a little tummy. But sometimes Luke felt really fat. That's when he felt like his mother. She was a Fuller Figure model. On one of her posters it said, "Fat is beautiful, too."

"Does Tracy think I'm good-looking?" thought Luke.

"I'll always be there for you, son," Luke's dad said.

"I know," said Luke and ate his toast.

"Dad can be there for me now," thought Luke. "He makes my breakfast. But where's my dad when the bad boys come?"

The bad boys were terrible. And Matt was the worst of them. Matt was the leader of the bad boys. And Matt was Tracy's boyfriend! Hand in hand, Tracy and Matt walked around school together every day.

Luke felt ill when he thought about Matt and Tracy kissing.

"Why Matt?" asked Luke. Of course Luke knew the answer. Matt was the best sportsman in school. Matt could do everything. He was suntanned. Matt was brown even in winter. Matt was in the rugby team. Matt was in the football team, too. And all the girls loved him – although he was a bastard.

Luke only loved Tracy. Luke wasn't suntanned. Luke wasn't even brown in the summer. Luke wasn't slim. Luke didn't play rugby. Luke only played football in the garden with his dad. Luke made music. And Luke's mother was a Fuller Figure model.

Luke walked slowly to the bus-stop. After five minutes the bus came. Matt was sitting on the bus. Matt always got on the bus two stops before Luke. All the other bad boys were already on the bus, too.

When Luke got on the bus, Matt shouted, "Hi, Fatty!" Luke didn't look at Matt. He put his hand in his backpack and got some headphones out. The journey to school was only OK if he listened to music.

"What are you listening to, Fatso?" Matt shouted so loud that Luke could hear him. "Is it 'Mighty Matt, Mega Man'?"

"Hey, Fatso, I'm talking to you!" Matt shouted. The bad boys were laughing.

Luke needed help. But nobody wanted to help him against terrible Matt. The group of boys with Matt was too big.

Matt and his friends made jokes about fat people, and Luke counted the stops to school. It was a terrible countdown, because Luke knew what all the kids in the bus would soon see.

Luke's mother was on a poster near St John's Church. On the poster she was wearing a terrible dress. Everybody could see that Luke's mother wasn't slim.

Of course Luke was proud of his mother. Again and again he saw her on posters, in magazines, often on TV, too. Luke's dad said that his mother was the most famous Fuller Figure model

in England. That's why it was easy for the bad boys to make jokes about her.
But when the bus reached St John's Church the poster was gone.
"Hey, where has your mother gone, Fatso?" shouted Matt.
Luke wanted to hit Matt. But Matt was too strong for that. And hitting somebody didn't solve problems. You had to talk about things. But you couldn't talk to Matt. He was a really bad, bad boy.
Eddy got on at the next stop. Eddy lived so near to school he could really walk. But Eddy couldn't see very well. His glasses were like church windows.
"Hey, Four Eyes!" shouted Matt.
Eddy went pale. Matt was sitting with his friends at the back of the bus. Eddy couldn't see that far. But he could hear Matt's "song":

Four Eyes, Four Eyes,
Your glasses are the wrong size.
Four Eyes, Four Eyes,
You'll never win a beauty prize!

Luke got up and spoke to Eddy. "Come and sit with me, Eddy," he said quietly.
"Hallo, Luke, it's good to see you."
"Fatso and Four Eyes, ha ha!" the boys at the back shouted. "Fat and blind!"
"If you aren't quiet now, boys, you'll have to get off my bus," said a voice from the loudspeakers.
The bad boys stopped laughing. They stopped shouting bad words. When the bus stopped in front of the school, Eddy and Luke jumped up. They were soon out of the bus. Together with

lots of other students they went towards the school. It was an old school. The walls were red and the windows were big.

"Thanks, Luke," Eddy said when they went their different ways. Eddy wasn't in Luke's class any more now. Two years earlier Eddy repeated a class. Luke never understood how this could happen. Eddy was a really clever boy.

"No problem," said Luke. "Bye!" Just at that moment it happened. Luke crashed into somebody. It all happened very fast. Suddenly Luke was lying on the floor. A few older students were laughing.

"Can't you be careful?" a girl asked angrily.

"Tr-Tr-Tracy, I'm so sorry!"

"Look, all my felt-tips are on the floor."

"I d-d-didn't do it on p-p-purpose."

"Luke, I didn't know you stammered," said Tracy, as she started to pick up her felt-tips.

"I don't st-st-stammer," said Luke, as he helped Tracy.

"Well, it sounds like stammering to me!" said Tracy.

"I rap," said Luke.

"What do you do?"

"Oh no," thought Luke. "Now it has come out. I've told Tracy that I rap. Almost nobody knows that I want to be a musician, a really big rap star."

Only Luke's best friends knew his secret. Of course his parents knew about it, too. And Mr Harrison, the music teacher.

"Do you really rap?" asked Tracy.

Luke nodded and went red. "Yes," he said.

"That's great," said Tracy.

"Really?" Luke asked. He couldn't believe this. He was next to Tracy. And Tracy was speaking to him! She thought it was great that he rapped. Wow!

"Can you rap something for me?" asked Tracy.

Luke shook his head.

"Don't you want to?"

"I have to go to my lesson now."

"Yes, of course. You're right." Tracy looked at her watch. Luke's heart missed a few beats. Tracy looked fantastic. Her hair, her eyes. And her hands. He'd really like to hold her hands – now!

With a dry throat he said, "Why don't you come to my first concert?"

"You're giving a concert?"

Luke nodded proudly. "In a month."

"Great!"

Luke put his hand in his backpack and looked for a ticket.

"Here you are," he said. "It's just a small concert in a youth club."
"Great!" Tracy beamed.
"But there are two tickets," Tracy said.
"Oh," said Luke. "Er, ... yes."
"So I can bring somebody then?" asked Tracy.
"Yes," said Luke. "Silly! Silly! Silly!" he thought. "Why did you give her two tickets? Please, please, please! Not Matt. Please, please, please!"
"I'll bring my friend Carol," said Tracy and got up. She had all her felt-tips except one. The missing felt-tip was red. Luke had it in his hand!
"You're coming then?" asked Luke.
"With Carol. Yes."
At that moment Luke was the happiest boy in the whole school.

CHAPTER TWO

On the next days Luke loved getting up. He was awake before the alarm clock. With open eyes he went on dreaming his dream. Tracy was standing behind her window. She was smiling at him. He smiled back. Sometimes he dreamed of his show. Tracy was in front of the stage. She was listening to his songs and dancing to his words. Luke saw the happiness in her eyes. "Will it ever happen?" he asked himself. "Yes, yes!" a voice inside him said.

The bus journey to school wasn't too bad any more for Luke. Of course Matt and his friends still annoyed him. Bad boys just can't stop that.

"What's the matter, son?" Mr Layton asked on Friday morning.

"Nothing, Dad."

"Nothing?"

"Really, nothing," answered Luke.

"The way you're smiling, a lot is the matter with you. And you're singing much more than usual. You even sing when you do your homework!"

Luke shook his head. "No, Dad. That isn't right! When I do my homework, I don't think about my music. I think about history, geography and about the fantastic world of numbers – maths."

Luke's dad laughed. "You're OK, son."

Luke went red. His dad was right. Of course he was OK. But his dad was right, too, about Luke singing a lot – even when he was doing his homework. It was a new song that he was singing. He was still writing it. In the evening, when he lay in bed, he had his writing block on his knees. With Tracy's red felt-tip he worked on his new song, "I am what I am". The song was about Luke Layton – and love.

Did Tracy love him …?

Luke didn't worry now when Matt said silly things. "Love makes me strong," he thought.

Eddy wasn't so lucky. Every time Matt said something silly, he felt terrible.

"Sit next to me," Luke said to the boy with glasses one day on the bus.

"Thanks, Luke."

"Just don't listen," said Luke.

"It's easy for you," answered Eddy.

"If you don't listen, the words won't hurt you," said Luke.

Eddy looked at Luke's discman. "You mean I should listen to music, so that I can't hear Matt and his friends?"

Luke nodded.

"But then I won't hear anything else."

"Everything has its price," Luke said. "And the price isn't always nice."

"Nice? Oh, no! Now I remember!" Eddy put his hand to his head.

"What do you remember?" asked Luke.

"You know Constance?"

"Conny? In Year 9?"

"Yes, Conny."

"What's the matter with Conny?"

" I heard something," Eddy said.

"What did you hear?" Luke was getting curious.

Constance was a friend of Tracy's. They went to the same ballet school. Luke thought Conny was good-looking, but she wasn't as nice as Tracy. Tracy was fantastic, Conny was just great.

"I heard her and Tracy talking. You know Tracy, don't you?"

Luke went red. Of course he knew Tracy. He loved Tracy.

"They were talking about you!" Eddy said and laughed.

"What did they say? What did they say?" Luke asked.

"Conny said that you can't dance," said Eddy.

"Silly cow!" said Luke.

"And Tracy said that you're a nice boy."

"Nice? What did she mean? Did she explain it?"

"You're different from the other boys, she said," said Eddy. "I am what I am," answered Luke. And suddenly the next verse of his "I am what I am"-rap was in his head. He didn't have to write it down. He couldn't forget these words …

I'm a nice boy, man,
I do what I can.
I can't dance, but I sing,
My song is everything.
My girl says I'm the best,
I'm not like the rest.
I'm a nice boy, man,
I am what I am.

The next weekend Luke worked very hard on his show. He spent Saturday morning at the youth club. Mr Smythe went through the evening with him, every song. Where should which light shine, and when? They used the fog machine three times. Luke needed it for the rap "Foggy Robby". Robby only wore grey clothes. Robby was as grey as fog, his friends said. And everybody thought that Robby loved the fog. But Robby was really very frightened of fog. He was frightened of everything. Life was one big fog for Robby.

When I walk, when I jog,
I only see fog.
The fog is my breath,
My life is like death.

Without the fog the song wasn't as frightening as Luke wanted it to be.

"What's the matter with you, Luke?" asked Mr Smythe.
"I'm in love, Mr Smythe," Luke answered proudly.
"And is she in love with you?" Mr Smythe wanted to know.
"She's coming to my show," Luke said.
"OK then, let's give your big love a super show," said Mr Smythe.

On Wednesday it happened. Tracy asked Luke a question.
"Where's my red felt-tip?" she said.
"Good morning, Tracy," said Luke.
"Only you can have the felt-tip," said Tracy. Her face didn't look as angry as her words sounded.
"Perhaps," Luke said.
Tracy hit Luke in the side. It felt like lightning to Luke.
"I'll look at home," Luke said.
"Yes, please. And then bring the felt-tip to my house," said Tracy.
Luke and Tracy looked into each other's eyes. They went red. They didn't run into their classrooms till they heard the second bell. Their hearts were beating very fast – and not only because they were running …

Of course Luke knew that he had Tracy's red felt-tip. But he knew that he could only write his "I am what I am"-rap with that felt-tip. So after his homework he went on working on his rap. Word after word appeared as if by magic in his writing block. After only an hour the song was finished.

I'm not big, I'm not small,
I'm not slim, I'm not tall.
I'm a regular guy.
I laugh and I cry.

I like what I do
And I do what I like.
I am what I am
Now get on your bike.

I'm a nice boy, man,
I do what I can.
I can't dance, but I sing,
My song is everything.
My girl says I'm the best,
I'm not like the rest
I'm a nice boy, man,
I am what I am.

North, south, east, west,
My girl is the best.
Tomorrow, today,
I see her every day.
She has a face like a dream.
All peaches and cream.
She is what she is,
Makes my heart go whizz.

I am what I am,
She likes what she sees.
I want to be your man,
Oh Tracy, come on, please!
I'll give you my heart
And the stars above.
I am what I am,
Let me give you my love.

On Thursday Luke's dream came true. He was standing in front of Tracy's house. He looked up at her window. His heart was beating fast and his fingers were gripping the red felt-tip. "Please, please," he thought. "Please come to the window."
A few minutes later, when Tracy appeared at the window, Luke's heart almost exploded with happiness. His knees shook as he walked up to the door and rang the bell.
"Ding," went the bell. Then "Dong".
"Hallo, Luke," Tracy said and beamed at him.
"Hallo, Tracy," Luke said.
"It's nice of you to bring my felt-tip. Would you like some tea?" asked Tracy.
"Yes, please."

This wasn't the only "teatime" that Luke had at Tracy's house. In the next two weeks he visited Tracy as often as he could. Luke talked about so many different things with Tracy.
"You're so different," Tracy often said.
"I am what I am," answered Luke.
"Yes," Tracy nodded. "And that's good."
They both talked about music, of course. Luke could talk a lot about music. But when Tracy talked about herself, Luke listened. He was interested in what Tracy told him. Luke listened when Tracy talked about ballet. Tracy loved ballet dancing.
"Can you teach me?" Luke asked one day.
Tracy laughed and shook her head.
"If you really want to, I can try."

But when Luke tried his first pirouette between Tracy's bed and her cupboard, he fell so hard that Tracy's parents wanted to take Luke to hospital.

"No, thank you," he said. "I haven't hurt myself."

On the next days Tracy and Luke did safer things in their free time. They ate ice-cream, they went by bus to the park and talked and talked and talked.
"Matt doesn't do this with me," said Tracy.
"Oh, yes, Matt." Luke suddenly felt very sad. Tracy was still Matt's girl.
"You're so different from Matt."
"Of course I'm different," thought Luke.
"You listen to me," said Tracy.
Luke put his arm around her.
"You take me seriously," said Tracy.
"Well, I ...," said Luke.
"Even when I was talking about my Uncle Stan's flowers, you listened."
"I thought it was interesting," said Luke.
"You're interesting," said Tracy.
"And Matt?"
After some time Tracy said, "Matt is interesting too. But only in his own way, of course."

Luke still had to work hard on his first show. His future depended on this show. He was sure of this. Not only his future as a musician, but his future at Tracy's side, too. Luke was sure that he could win Tracy's heart with his show. And he could take a big step up on the career ladder.

Two days before his first show Bad Matt was waiting for him. The boy was standing in front of the door of Luke's classroom. His hands were fists, in front of his chest.
"Hallo, Luke, my friend," said Matt.

Luke was so surprised he couldn't answer.

"Tracy has told me a lot about you," Matt said and smiled.

"What has she told you?" Luke asked cautiously. You couldn't trust boys like Matt.

"You sing operas," Matt said.

"No, not operas," Luke said.

"That's good," answered Matt.

"Really! Operas! I could never sing anything so boring."

"Great," said Matt. "I don't like operas or opera singers."

"I hate them, too," answered Luke.

"Why did Tracy tell me something different?"

"I don't know." Luke really didn't know.

"And you really don't sing operas?" Matt wasn't sure.
"Look, come to my first show," Luke said.
"Wow!" Matt sounded surprised. "You give shows?"
"Yes," said Luke proudly.
"And you won't sing operas?" asked Matt.
Luke laughed. "I don't even know how to spell the word 'opera'."
"Luke," said Matt and put his hand on Luke's shoulder. "Luke, my old friend, I believe you – almost. So sing something for me."
"Oh, no," thought Luke. Which of his songs should he sing to Matt? He had so many good songs. They were songs about boys and girls who were so different from Matt and his friends. There was that rap about Robby. But he was sure that he couldn't sing Matt a song about a frightened boy. Boys were only boys for Matt if they were tough. "Matt will never be my fan," thought Luke. His songs were full of boys and girls who were unsure of themselves. It was all to do with puberty, Luke's dad said. But what did Luke's dad know about puberty?
"Where can I get a ticket for your first show?" said Matt.
"I'll give you a ticket," said Luke.
"You're a real friend," said Matt.
He said this again when Luke gave him the ticket for his first show. Then he said, "I'm looking forward to it."
"Really?" asked Luke.
"Yes," said Matt. "I'm really sorry I was often so nasty to you."
"That's nice of you to say that," said Luke. "See you at the show, Matt!"

CHAPTER THREE

There was no music lesson at school on Friday. Mr Harrison was ill for the next two weeks. Luke was happy about the free lesson, but he was sad, too. Now Mr Harrison couldn't come to his first show. Mr Harrison was a great teacher. He told Luke again and again that music was more than just standing in front of a microphone and singing something. Music was art.

As Luke went out of the classroom, Stevie came towards him. Stevie was in Luke's class. The two boys sat at the same table. Stevie was good at geography. Luke's best subject – after music – was maths. As often as they could, they helped each other with homework.

"I can come after all," shouted Stevie.

"Wow!"

"My mother isn't going to visit her sister!"

Luke was happy. Stevie often had to look after his younger sister when his mother was away.

"Girls are silly," Stevie often said, and Luke always shook his head. "Not all girls!"

"Hey, Luke, what are you dreaming about?"

"I'm nervous!" Luke said.

"About your show?"

"Yes, that, too."

"What do you mean – that, too?"

"Er, well, er ...," said Luke.

"You're in love," Stevie said.

"Yes, I am." Luke went red.

"Who is it?"

"I'm not telling you," said Luke.

Luke patted Stevie on the shoulder. "See you tonight," he said.

"Hey!" Stevie shouted.

"See you tonight!" Luke shouted.

"Who are you in love with?" shouted Stevie.

Luke put his head down and ran out of school. He loved Tracy, but the whole world didn't have to know about his love. Tonight was his night! He was going to sing his song! With a beating heart, Luke looked forward to his show.

The youth club was on the corner of Exeter Avenue and Devon Street. When Luke got out of the bus, Mrs Hemingway was standing at the door. Mrs Hemingway was the youth club leader. She was about 30 years old. She always wore leather trousers and black T-shirts. Mrs Hemingway was great. The whole club was great. The young people at the club didn't even mind Mr Smythe. In their eyes he was a really old man. He was over 50! Mr Smythe looked after technical things at the youth club. On disco evenings he put the music on. And he always checked that there was enough cola and lemonade.

"Hallo, Mrs Hemingway," said Luke.

"Is everything OK, Luke?" Mrs Hemingway asked.

Luke shook his head. It was the day of his first show. He was going to sing his songs to a large audience. All his friends were going to come. And lots of other boys and girls, too. All over this part of town there were signs with his name. On the posters it said "Lucky Luke", and under this it said "Rapper". One of these posters was next to the club door. "That's me," thought Luke.

Two hours later Luke was standing very nervously behind the small stage. The youth club was full. Luke went through the list of his songs again. The last song on the list was "I am what I am." Luke wanted to keep the best till the end of the show.

"You'll be OK, son," said Mr Smythe and patted him on the shoulder.

"I'm OK," said Luke. But he didn't feel OK. He was very nervous. He couldn't even think of the words he wanted to say before he started singing. That's what all big stars did. They said hallo to the audience.

Mr Smythe looked at his watch. "One more minute!"

Sixty seconds! That was the title of his fifth song. It was about a boy who had sixty seconds to …

Luke was so nervous! What was "Sixty seconds" about?!

"Stage fright?" asked Mr Smythe.

Luke nodded. His throat was dry. And there was nothing in his head. Luke didn't know anything any more.

"It'll go away," laughed Mr Smythe and went into his corner.

Luke wanted to run home. His first show!

Then Luke heard Mrs Hemingway's voice: "He's young. He's good. He's Lucky Luke."

Applause.

"Today. Here. For you!"

Applause.

"The applause is for me," thought Luke.

"Let's all give a warm welcome to Luke!"

The applause got louder.

"The one and only Lucky Luke!" shouted Mrs Hemingway.

Luke took a deep breath. He didn't feel lucky. He felt terrible. There was still something in his throat.

"Go on, Luke! You're on!" said Mrs Hemingway.

Luke closed his eyes, then opened them again. He walked onto the stage.
"Hi," he said.
Applause.
"Hallo, all you guys. It's time to get wise, time for a surprise. It's Luke time, Lucky Luke time!"
In his corner Mr Smythe started the music. And with every beat Luke felt better and better. His throat felt OK. When the big red light started to shine, Luke started to rap.
His first song was "Solidarity".

Four songs later Luke was happy. The audience was on his side. And Tracy was standing in front of the stage. The girl was beaming at him. She was following everything he said. As often as he could, Luke looked at her. She was wearing a red dress. It was the same red as the felt-tip.

Then it happened. Somebody whistled. Luke was so startled he almost forgot what to sing. Angrily he looked into the audience. All the boys and girls were moving to the beat of the music. No, not all of them! Luke shook his head as he sang, "No, man, I know her. I follow this girl. No, man, ..."
Luke was shaking his head because of the boys near Matt. They weren't moving with the beat of the music. They were just looking angrily at Luke. And then Matt moved two fingers towards his mouth. And then he whistled – long and loud. The other bad boys started whistling, too.
Luke was so startled that he sang, "No, Matt, I know her, I love this girl ..."
"Stop singing operas!" shouted Matt.
One of the boys from the group applauded his leader. Another boy shouted loudly, "Boo!"

Luke stopped singing. He had to get everybody quiet. This was his first show. He didn't want Matt and his friends to ruin it.

"Please, friends," he said, as the music went on playing. "Please be quiet."

"Go on singing, Luke!" a girl's voice shouted from the audience. Was it Tracy's voice? Luke was sure it was.

"Friends, please!"

"I'm not your friend!" shouted Matt.

"Fatty Luke!" shouted one of Matt's friends.

"Fatty Luke sings funny operas!" shouted Matt.

Some other people repeated Matt's nasty words.

"Shut up!" Luke shouted into his microphone. That was the title of the song that was just starting.

Matt and his friends laughed. "Wow!" they shouted. "How tough Fatty Luke can sound!"

Luke went on singing. "Shut up!" His friends sang the chorus with him. Stevie sang loudly, too. The boy was standing next to Matt and his gang.

"How much does your mother weigh?" Matt shouted.

Luke was really very angry. But he went on singing.

Out of the corner of his eye Luke saw Mr Smythe. He was shaking his head. He had his phone in his hand.

The bad boys had football whistles now. Nobody could hear the music. Stevie was making fists.

Just before Luke's friend could hit Matt, Mr Smythe put the loudspeakers on full power and the music got louder. The loudspeakers sounded terrible now. When Luke sang "lucky", it sounded like "lady". Matt thought this was really funny.

"Lady Luke!" he shouted. There he was, in front of the stage. Behind him were his silly friends.

Luke's friends were in a group, too.

"Please, friends, please!" Luke shouted.

"Come on, Fatty. You can't be happy. You're a big Fatty. Your songs are so crappy!" Matt "rapped".

Suddenly the music stopped. Everything was quiet in the youth club, except "rapping" Matt.

"Why are you doing this, Matt?" asked Luke and put the microphone down. His first show was a disaster.

"Because you're singing operas!" Matt shouted.

"Shut up!" shouted Stevie and ran towards Matt and his friends. Three boys followed him. But there were too many of Matt's friends.

"Come down, Luke!" Matt said.

Luke shook his head.

"Are you frightened?"

"I'm a musician," said Luke.

"What? A musician? You're a coward. You hide behind words!"

"Better to hide behind words than to hide behind fists," said Luke.

Luke took a deep breath. Where was Tracy? The girl wasn't there. "Matt, you stupid bastard!" Luke thought. Just as he was about to jump down from the stage, all the lights in the youth club went on.

"What's happening?" asked Mrs Hemingway. The club leader was standing at the door.

Nobody said anything.

"This is a rap show, not a boxing match," she said.

"Luke is really crappy," said Matt.

"Nobody is crappy," said Mrs Hemingway and shook her head.

"*He* is," said Matt.

"Get out!" said Mrs Hemingway.

Matt stayed where he was.

"All of you, go! Now!" said Mrs Hemingway.

"No, please," said Luke. "No!"

"Oh yes," said Mrs Hemingway. "In this club there are rules. And everybody has to obey them. Everybody!"

"But Matt and his friends started it," said Luke.

"I'm not interested!" said Mrs Hemingway. She looked sad. She knew how important the show was to Luke.

People started to go. "We'll talk about this later," Stevie said to Matt.

"I'd like that, Stevie!" laughed Matt.

"Now get out!" said Mrs Hemingway. "All of you!"

An hour later Luke was standing at the bus-stop. The CDs in his bag weighed a ton. "Cheer up!" said Stevie. All Luke's other friends were at the bus-stop, too.
"Thanks, all of you," said Luke.
"Things will be OK," people said to him.
"There'll be another show."
"But will Tracy come next time?" Luke asked himself.
"What does she think of me? Does she still like me? She must think I'm a coward. I hid behind my microphone! These and other things went through Luke's head. His friends couldn't help him. Even Mrs Hemingway's promise didn't help. She said she had another date free for new musicians like Luke – in three months. Three months? What a long time! So much could happen in three months. He loved Tracy now, and she liked him. He had to show her who he was.

CHAPTER FOUR

Luke travelled around the city for an hour. Again and again he got on another bus. He didn't look at the bus numbers. He had to think. Sitting in a bus was perfect for this. The city went past him. He saw houses. He saw windows. And he saw people. The city was life. But he was far away from this life. The window of the bus was between him and the city. He saw his face in the glass. "What should I do?" Luke asked his face. He asked the city the same question.

The city answered him in long sentences. The city talked of love. Luke saw couples. Some of the couples were young, some were old. Some of the couples were hand in hand, some weren't. Luke saw a woman running after a man. Luke saw a couple arguing. "You are you," the city said. "And you are good!"

"But I'm not good enough," Luke said to his face in the window. "I can't even give a concert!"

When Luke came home, his father wasn't there. "I'm getting pizzas," a note said. "Back soon!" Mr Layton was back five minutes later.

"How did it go?" he asked. In his hands he had two very big pizza boxes.

Luke started to cry.

"Oh, Luke, what happened?"

Luke told his dad the whole story.

Luke and his dad talked till late at night. They didn't eat the pizzas. Sometimes there were more important things than hunger.

Luke went to his room at two o'clock. He listened to "I am what I am" on his stereo.
He wanted to sing this song to Tracy. Now he had to listen to it alone. Luke remembered his dad's words. "OK, son, it didn't work today. Then it will just have to work tomorrow!" Was his dad right? Was there a second chance for him? Or was Tracy lost forever?

On Saturday Luke went to see his mother. It was "her" weekend. In the week Luke lived with his dad. At the weekends his parents took turns. His parents were OK. He was happy to live with his father, but it was good to see his mother often, too. He often phoned her and talked about his problems, big and small. That's what mothers were for. Of course Luke talked about problems with his dad, too. That's what parents were for. Luke loved his parents. The fact that his parents didn't love each other couldn't change that.

Luke arrived at his mum's house in time for breakfast.
"I have some sausages," his mother said.
"Wow!"
"And there are beans, too."
"Great!"
Of course Luke's mother asked about his show.
"Aren't you going to tell me what it was like?"
Luke's sausage almost stuck in his throat. He coughed.
"What happened?"
Luke said nothing.
"Didn't Tracy come?" she asked.
"Yes, she did," said Luke.
"Didn't she like your music?"
"I don't know," Luke said.

"And that's your problem?"

Luke shook his head. He looked at his plate.

"Look at me, Luke."

Luke looked at his plate.

"Luke," his mother said and leaned towards him.

Luke looked at her. He saw her love. He suddenly had an idea for a new song – "Mother's Eyes".

"What happened?" his mother asked.

Luke told her everything.

"Have you talked to your dad about this?"

"Yes."

"And what did he say?"

"He said I should talk to you about it, too," said Luke.

"Is that all he said?" Luke's mum asked.

Luke shook his head.

"Love is nice," said Luke's mum. "But love is terrible, too. Do you know about lovesickness?"

Luke nodded.

"Luke, lovesickness isn't worth it."

"It isn't?"

"Lovesickness can make you ill."

Luke nodded.

"What's nice about being ill?" his mother asked.

"Nothing."

"So why are you lovesick?" his mother asked.

"It's all so difficult!" Luke groaned. And he thought about the show and about Matt. He could never win against Matt. Matt looked good. He always wore the most expensive clothes. Matt could have the girls he wanted. And Tracy was Matt's girl. Tracy looked good, too. No, Tracy always looked *great*! Tracy could have the boys she wanted. And Matt was her boyfriend.

"What's so difficult?" Luke's mother asked after a while.

"I can't give Tracy anything," Luke said.
"Yes, you can," his mother said.
"But what?" Luke shouted and pushed his breakfast plate away.
"You!"
"Me?"
"Yes, Luke."
"But what am I?"
"You're you," his mother said.
Luke shook his head. "Yes, I'm me. I'm not good at sport. I wear old jeans. I'm not slim. I'm bad at geography. I have big feet. And I often have bad breath. And I'm frightened of boys like Matt."
"Luke, you are you," his mother said. This time Luke didn't look away.
"Lots of boys aren't good at sport. So what! Your dad wasn't good at sport. And he wore glasses. But we were still a couple!"
"But you aren't a couple any more!"
Luke's mum shook her head. "That's another story. We were very happy for many years. Even if happiness doesn't stay happiness, that doesn't make it bad."
Luke didn't really understand what his mother was trying to tell him. But he nodded.
"Everybody is special," his mother said.
"But the concert failed. Matt ruined it. Mrs Hemingway sent everybody home. Tracy left without saying goodbye to me."
"Luke, Luke, Luke!" His mother looked at him and shook her head.
Luke's mum got up. She stood next to her boy. She held his shoulders. "Sometimes you win, sometimes you lose. You often can't do anything about the failures. But you can fight and win next time. Don't give up. You must talk to your girl."

My girl? That sounded great. That was just what Luke wanted to hear.

"Fight for her!" his mother said.

Luke looked at his fists. They were small.

"Show her you're strong," his mother said.

"Matt is much stronger than me!"

"Can Matt sing?"

Luke laughed. "No, Mum, he can't."

"But you can! That's where you're strong and I'm proud of you."

Luke remembered the year his mother started as a model. He was ten years old at the time. A photographer talked to his mother in the street. Mrs Layton thought the offer of a trial shoot was a joke. She couldn't believe that people wanted her as a model. She was 1.70 metres tall and she weighed 75 kilos. Models were slim. And they were young. Luke's mum was 33 at the time. Today his mum was a famous model. "Slim I'm not, So what!" That was what she said. She thought her kilos were OK. "I am what I am," his mother always said. "I wouldn't like to be different."

"Will you fight?" his mum asked.

Luke nodded.

"I can't hear you."

"Yes...," he said quietly.

"Is that what fighters sound like?"

Luke shook his head.

"What do fighters sound like?"

Luke got up.

"I am what I am!" he shouted. And then he rapped Tracy's song for his mother. There was a new verse at the end.

I am what I am
And I know what is right.
I'm tough and I'm strong,
I know I can fight.
I fight with my words,
I fight with my song.
If you think I can't fight,
Oh, man, you're so wrong!

Luke's mum clapped loudly, then she said, "I'll be back in an hour. I have to look after the flowers for a friend. She's on holiday."

Luke was grateful to his mum for going out. Now he could phone Tracy. He had an hour.

"872545," said a man's voice.

"Hi, it's me, Luke. Is Tracy there?"

"Luke?"

"Lucky Luke."

"Oh, *that* Luke," said Tracy's dad.

Luke liked Tracy's dad. He collected comics. He had all the Lucky Luke comics. In five different languages. Luke thought about the comics. Was Matt one of the Daltons? Were the bad boys the Dalton Gang? But Luke was Lucky Luke. He could sing faster than his shadow.

"Tracy Brown."

"Hallo, Tracy. It's me, Luke."

"Oh, Luke, thanks for phoning."

Luke almost dropped the telephone.

"Did you get home OK yesterday?" Luke asked.

"Yes, thanks for asking."

"I was worried about you."

"About me?"

"Yes, Tracy."

"Oh, Luke."

"You suddenly left the youth club."

"Oh, Luke. I was so angry."

Luke went pale.

"Matt is such a bastard! He ruined your show!"

"Yes, he did."

"I'm very sorry for you."

"I'll be OK," said Luke.

"You're a nice guy," said Tracy.

Luke's heart was beating fast. "And you're a nice girl," he said.

"It's my birthday in three weeks," said Tracy.

"Oh, is it?" said Luke. Of course he knew when Tracy's birthday was. He knew almost everything about Tracy. He was in love with the girl.

"I'd like to invite you to my party," she said.

"Thank you, Tracy."

"Does that mean you'll come?"

Luke wasn't sure, but he thought Tracy's voice sounded a little hesitant. She was almost stammering!

"Luke? Will you come?"

"Yes," he said. "Yes, I'd love to."

"Great!"

Luke was very happy. "What would you like for your birthday?" he asked.

"A rap."

"What did you say?" asked Luke.

"Please, Luke. Write a rap for me! Sing me a song. Rap on my birthday!"

CHAPTER FIVE

Luke's alarm clock rang. He opened his eyes. The birds were singing outside the windows. The sun was shining into his room. "It's Saturday," thought Luke. "It's my Saturday."
He jumped out of bed and ran into the bathroom. He sang an old pop song under the shower. It was Luke's parents' favourite song. Luke didn't really like pop songs. But today everything was different.
Then he went downstairs to the kitchen.
"What's the matter with you, Luke?" asked his father.
Luke went on singing.
"Is Matt coming, too?" Luke's father asked.
"No, he isn't!" Luke shouted. "I'm so happy! Tracy hasn't invited Matt."
"That's good, Luke."
"It's over between the two of them."
"Great!"
"Tracy says that Matt is a bastard."
"And is he?"
"You know he is."
"Then nothing can go wrong," said Luke's dad.

But something almost did go wrong. Mr Layton's car didn't start. And father and son wanted to go to town. Luke needed some new trousers and a new shirt. "If you sing well, you have to look good, too," his dad said.
So they went by bus. And that took longer. They had to change buses. And the same on the way home. But Luke didn't mind.

In his shopping bags he had not only some new trousers and a new shirt, but some really cool shoes, too.

At two o'clock Luke was standing on the street corner. On the other side of the street was the house that Tracy lived in. Luke looked up at her window. Tracy's face appeared at the window. Luke waved to his girl. Tracy waved back. She opened the door.

"It's great to see you," she said.

"Is that a new hairstyle?" asked Luke.

"Yes," said Tracy and smiled. "You notice everything."

Her beautiful hair wasn't tied back today. Her lips were red. And she was wearing make-up.

"C-Can I come in?" Luke stammered.

"Yes, of course," laughed Tracy.

"Is the big star here?" Tracy's mother shouted from the kitchen.

"Yes, Mum."

Luke went red. "I'm not big," he said.

"No, but you're a star!" Tracy looked at him with shining eyes.

"No, no!" Luke shook his head. But Tracy's words made him very happy.

"But you'll be a star one day," Tracy said.

"Yes, of course," Luke said and smiled.

Tracy leaned towards Luke. "You're already my star today," she whispered.

Tracy's mum came out of the kitchen. "Hallo, Luke," she said. "Would you like something to drink? Lemonade, cola, orange juice?"

"Thank you, Mrs Brown. I'd like a cola."

The garden looked fantastic. There was a big table with lots of food on it. Salads, sandwiches, cold sausages on sticks, cheese and pineapple on sticks, chicken legs and lots of other things were waiting for the guests. Next to the food table there were some small garden tables and chairs. And on the other side of the garden there were some boards on bricks …

Mr Brown was standing behind the barbecue.
"Hallo, Luke," he said.
"Hallo, Mr Brown."
"What are you going to sing for us today? Is it …?"
"Oh, John. Tracy has told us again and again about Luke's songs," Mrs Brown said.
"You know music isn't my thing. I can't remember all the song titles. Especially not all the modern things."
"Luke doesn't do modern things," said Tracy and held Luke's hand. Luke went red. Tracy often held his hand now, but never in front of her parents.
"OK, OK," Mr Brown said to his daughter. "I'll shut up. And I'll put some nice things for you all on the barbecue."

The party started at three o'clock. Most guests knew Luke from school. Girls and boys from Tracy's class came and friends from her street, too. And, of course, some girls from Tracy's ballet class were there, too. There were almost 30 boys and girls in the garden. And they were all hungry. Mr Brown couldn't cook as fast as they all ate. And Mrs Brown was busy, too. She kept bringing drinks to everybody. The Browns really looked after their guests well.

Suddenly Matt arrived! In his hand he had a present. He was dressed well. He was even wearing a jacket.

When Tracy saw her ex-boyfriend, she jumped up from her chair. Luke held her hand. "Tracy," he said. "Tracy, please!"

"What's he doing here?" the girl said angrily.

"Please, Tracy." Now Luke got up.

"He'll ruin my party," said Tracy.

"Perhaps he wants to say sorry to you," Luke said.

"He should say sorry to *you,*" said Tracy. "He ruined your show."

"That was three weeks ago," Luke said. "I just want to forget it. Other things are so much more important." He looked at Tracy.

She leaned so close to Luke that he could smell her hair.

"Perhaps you're right," she said.

At the beginning Matt behaved almost perfectly. With a hot dog in one hand and a present in the other, he came up to Tracy.

"It's good to see you," Matt said.

"I, er, ...," Tracy started and bit her lip. "It's good to see you, too."

"Look, I've brought you something," Matt said and held out the hot dog to Tracy. "Oh, I'm sorry, that's mine. This is for you." He gave Tracy the present. It was a CD: "Best of Opera".

Tracy wasn't sure if this was Matt's idea of a joke, so she just said, "Thanks, Matt."

Then Mrs Brown appeared.

"I didn't know you were invited, Matt."

"It's OK, Mum," said Tracy.

Later Matt became "Bad Matt" again. He told almost everybody at the party about Luke's failed show. And he told them about his part in the failure. Many of the guests already knew the story from Tracy, so they didn't think it was funny. Only some of the boys laughed. Perhaps they were laughing out of embarrassment. After all, Matt was Tracy's ex-boyfriend. And they all knew him.

Luke was going to start rapping at 6 o'clock. He was very nervous. "That's stage fright," said Mr Brown. The same thing always happens to me before a barbecue."

"Thanks, Mr Brown."

"Luke, I never knew why Tracy liked Matt. He's a loudmouth."

"He's good-looking," said Luke.

"Would you like another hot dog?" said Mr Brown and held out a plate to Luke. The sausage looked half-burnt.

"This sausage, for example, doesn't look good, but it tastes great! You won't find a better sausage! What's inside is important, Luke. What you are is the only thing that counts!"
"Thanks, Mr Brown," said Luke and took the sausage.

An hour later it was time. Luke had to get changed. He was still wearing jeans and a T-shirt. Tracy's parents said he could get changed in Tracy's bedroom. His bag with his new things was there. When Luke walked into the room, his heart missed a beat. There was a poster on Tracy's cupboard. "You're my star!" it said.
Luke was so happy. He almost ran back to the garden in the same clothes! But then he remembered why he was in Tracy's bedroom. He put on his new black trousers and white shirt. The shoes looked great with the new clothes. They were black and white checked.

A minute later Luke looked into the garden. Tracy was standing next to the CD-player. She was looking at the door. Luke waved. The show could start.
Tracy took the CD with the big summer hits out of the CD-player. All the guests looked at the birthday girl. Why was she taking the CD out in the middle of a song?
"He's young! He's good! He's Lucky Luke!"
Nobody knew what was happening. Luke's show was the birthday girl's secret.
"Today!" she shouted. "Here! For you! Let's all give a warm welcome to Luke!" Tracy beamed with happiness.
Now the guests understood what was happening and they applauded.
"The applause is for me," Luke thought.

"The one and only Lucky Luke!" Tracy shouted. And then she pressed PLAY on the CD-player.

Luke took a deep breath. He felt "lucky". It was all so different from his first show at the youth club. His love for Tracy gave him strength. She was his girl.

"Go on, Luke! You're on!" said Mr Brown.

Luke ran out of the house and through the garden. The guests looked at him in surprise. Luke heard somebody ask "Who is it?" Then Luke jumped onto the small, improvised stage and started to sing. His first song was "Solidarity".

After the first surprise Tracy's party guests clapped enthusiastically. Nobody had reckoned on this surprise. Not even Matt. The silly boy looked very pale as he stood next to the barbecue.

Luke sang as powerfully as he could. Today was his day. Today he could show everybody what he was made of. But above all, he could sing Tracy his song. He was especially looking forward to this.

Two songs later Matt was standing in front of the improvised stage. His hands were fists. His face was red with anger.

Luke only looked at Matt for a second. Today was his day!

"He's singing operas!" he shouted so that everybody could hear him.

Luke rapped as if his life depended on it.

"Look at the little boy!" Matt shouted.

"Be quiet!" a girl shouted. She was more than a lot smaller than Matt.

"*He* should be quiet," said Matt.

"No!" came from all over the garden.
"Shut up!" came from one corner.
"Just look at the little worm!" Matt shouted.
Luke looked at Tracy's parents. Mrs Brown was holding her husband back.
"He's crappy!" shouted Matt.
Luke started his next song. This was his day!
"He should go!" shouted Matt.
"No, you should go, Matt," Luke heard.
"Get out, Matt!"
"We don't want you here!"
"Shut up, Matt – now!"
Matt put his fists down. He couldn't win against the guests' solidarity. And he couldn't win against Luke's singing. Luke sang more and more powerfully. There was pure energy in his words.

Soon Matt was no longer standing in front of the stage. He was no longer even at the party. Luke was singing his song for Tracy. His rap was his message to the world about himself – and about his love for the girl who was looking up at him on his "stage".

I'm not big, I'm not small,
I'm not slim, I'm not tall.
I'm a regular guy.
I laugh and I cry.
I like what I do
And I do what I like.
I am what I am
Now get on your bike.

I'm a nice boy, man,
I do what I can.
I can't dance, but I sing,
My song is everything.
My girl says I'm the best,
I'm not like the rest
I'm a nice boy, man,
I am what I am.

North, south, east, west,
My girl is the best.
Tomorrow, today,
I see her every day.
She has a face like a dream.
All peaches and cream.
She is what she is,
Makes my heart go whizz.

I am what I am,
She likes what she sees.
I want to be your man,
Oh Tracy, come on, please!
I'll give you my heart
And the stars above.
I am what I am,
Let me give you my love.

I am what I am
And I know what is right.
I'm tough and I'm strong,
I know I can fight.

I fight with my words,
I fight with my song.
If you think I can't fight,
Oh, man, you're so wrong!

The end

VOCABULARY

Abbreviation: s.p. = simple past

A
about [ə'baʊt]: **he was about to jump** er war im Begriff zu springen
above [ə'bʌv]: **the stars above** die Sterne von oben
after ['ɑ:ftə]: **run after** hinterherrennen
after all [ɑ:ftə'rɔ:l] doch
against [ə'genst] gegen
alarm clock [ə'lɑ:mklʌk] Wecker
all [ɔ:l]: **it was all to do with puberty** das hatte alles mit der Pubertät zu tun
all over [ɔl'əʊvə] überall in
although [ɔ:l'ðəʊ] obwohl
annoy [ə'nɔɪ] ärgern
any ['eni]: **not ... any more** nicht mehr
appear [ə'pɪə] erscheinen
applaud [ə'plɔ:d] applaudieren, klatschen
applause [ə'plɔ:z] Beifall, Applaus
argue ['ɑ:gju:] (sich) streiten
around the city [ə'raʊnd] durch die Stadt
as [əz] als; **as if by magic** wie durch Zauberhand
audience ['ɔ:dɪəns] Publikum
awake [ə'weɪk]: **he was awake** er war wach

B
back [bæk]: **at the back of the bus** hinten im Bus
backpack ['bækpæk] Rucksack
ballet ['bæleɪ] Ballett
ballet dancing ['bæleɪdɑ:nsɪŋ] Balletttanz
barbecue ['bɑ:bɪkju:] Grill; Grillfest
bastard ['bɑ:stəd] Bastard (hier etwa: Schwein)
beam [bi:m] strahlen
beat [bi:t] **1.** schlagen; **2.** Rhythmus; Takt
beauty prize ['bju:tipraɪz] Schönheitspreis
behave [bɪ'heɪv] sich benehmen
bell [bel] Klingel; Läuten
bit [bɪt]: **she bit her lip** sie biss sich auf die Lippe
blind [blaɪnd] blind
board [bɔ:d] Brett
boxing match ['bɒksɪŋmætʃ] Boxkampf
breath [breθ] Atem; Atemzug
brick [brɪk] Ziegelstein, Backstein

C
career ladder [kə'rɪəlædə] Karriereleiter
cautious ['kɔ:ʃəs] vorsichtig
chance [tʃɑ:ns] Chance, Gelegenheit
change [tʃeɪndʒ] ändern; **change buses** umsteigen
checked [tʃekt] kariert
cheer [tʃɪə]: **Cheer up!** Kopf hoch!
chest [tʃest] Brust
chorus ['kɔ:rəs] Refrain
clap [klæp] (Beifall) klatschen
come true [kʌm'tru:] wahr werden
comic ['kɒmɪk] Comic(heft)
concert ['kɒnsət] Konzert
corner ['kɔ:nə] Ecke; Winkel
cough [kɒf] husten
could [kʊd] s.p. von **can**
couple ['kʌpl] Paar
coward ['kaʊəd] Feigling
crappy ['kræpi] beschissen
crash into somebody [kræʃ] mit jemandem zusammenstoßen
curious ['kjʊəriəs] neugierig

D
death [deθ] Tod
deep [di:p] tief
depend on [dɪ'pendɒn] abhängen von

disaster [dɪ'zɑ:stə] Desaster
divorced [dɪ'vɔ:st] geschieden
downstairs [daʊn'steəz] nach unten
dream [dri:m] **1.** träumen; **2.** Traum
dress [dres] Kleid
dressed [drest] angezogen
dry [draɪ] trocken

E
each other [i:tʃ'ʌðə] einander, sich
else [els]: **not ... anything else** sonst nichts mehr
embarrassment [ɪm'bærəsmənt] Verlegenheit
end [end] Ende
energy ['enədʒi] Energie, Kraft
enthusiastically [ɪnθju:zi'æstɪkli] begeistert
especially [ɪ'speʃəli] besonders
explode [ɪk'spləʊd] explodieren
eye [aɪ] Auge

F
face [feɪs] Gesicht
fact [fækt] Tatsache
fail [feɪl] scheitern
failure ['feɪljə] Misserfolg, Reinfall
fantastic [fæn'tæstɪk] fantastisch
fat [fæt] dick, fett
feet [fi:t] Füße
fight for [faɪt] kämpfen um
fighter ['faɪtə] Kämpfer/in
figure ['fɪgə] Figur
fist [fɪst] Faust
floor [flɔ:] Fußboden, Boden
fog [fɒg] Nebel
for [fɔ:]: **That's what they were for.** Dazu waren sie da.
forever [fər'evə] für immer (und ewig)
forward ['fɔ:wəd]: **look forward to** sich freuen auf
frightening ['fraɪtnɪŋ] beängstigend

G
get [get]: **Get out!** Raus!
get changed [get'tʃeɪndʒd] sich umziehen
glasses ['glɑ:sɪz] Brille
go on [gəʊ'ɒn] angehen; **Go on.** Komm schon! **go on doing something** etwas weiter tun
go pale/red [gəʊ'peɪl, geʊ'red] blass/rot werden
good-looking [gʊd'lʊkɪŋ] gut aussehend
grateful ['greɪtfl] dankbar
grey [greɪ] grau
grip [grɪp] umklammern
groan [grəʊn] stöhnen
guest [gest] Gast
guy [gaɪ] Typ

H
hair [heə] Haar, Haare
hairstyle ['heəstaɪl] Frisur
half-burnt [hɑ:f'bɜ:nt] halb verbrannt
happiness ['hæpɪnəs] Glück, Zufriedenheit
head [hed] Kopf
headphones ['hedfəʊnz] Kopfhörer
heart [hɑ:t] Herz
held [held] s.p. von **hold**
hesitant ['hezɪtənt] unsicher
hid [hɪd] s.p. von **hide**
hide [haɪd] (sich) verstecken
hit [hɪt] schlagen
hold [həʊld] halten
hold out [həʊld'aʊt] hinhalten
hurry up [hʌri'ʌp] sich beeilen
hunger ['hʌŋgə] Hunger

I
I'd love to. [aɪd'lʌvtu:] Sehr gern.
idea [aɪ'dɪə]: **his idea of a joke** seine Vorstellung von einem Scherz
if [ɪf] ob
improvised ['ɪmprəvaɪzd] improvisiert
in his own way [ɪnhɪz'əʊnweɪ] auf seine eigene Art
inside [ɪn'saɪd] innerhalb (von); innen, drinnen
invite [ɪn'vaɪt] einladen

J
jacket ['dʒækɪt] Jacket
jog [dʒɒg] joggen
just [dʒʌst] nur; einfach

K
keep doing something [ki:p] mit etwas weitermachen
kilo ['ki:ləʊ] Kilo

L
language ['læŋgwɪdʒ] Sprache
leader ['li:də] Anführer/in; Leiter/in
lean [li:n] sich lehnen
leather ['leðə] Leder
life [laɪf] Leben
lightning ['laɪtnɪŋ] Blitz
lip [lɪp] Lippe
little ['lɪtl] klein
look forward to [lʊk'fɔ:wədtə] sich freuen auf
lost [lɒst] verloren
loudmouth ['laʊdmaʊθ] Großmaul
loudspeaker [laʊd'spi:kə] Lautsprecher
love [lʌv] **1.** lieben, sehr mögen; **2.** Liebe; **I'm in love** ich bin verliebt
lovesick ['lʌvsɪk]: **you're lovesick** du hast Liebeskummer
lovesickness ['lʌvsɪknəs] Liebeskummer

M
machine [mə'ʃɪ:n] Maschine
magic ['mædʒɪk]: **as if by magic** wie durch Zauberhand
makes my heart go whizz [meɪks, wɪz] bringt mein Herz zum Zischen
me [mi:] ich; **It's me, Luke.** Hier spricht Luke.
microphone ['maɪkrəfəʊn] Mikrofon
middle ['mɪdl] Mitte
mighty ['maɪti] mächtig
mind [maɪnd]: **they didn't mind him** sie hatten nichts gegen ihn
mine [maɪn] meine/r/s
miss a few beats [mɪs, bi:ts] ein paar Takte aussetzen
mouth [maʊθ] Mund
move [mu:v] (sich) bewegen
musician [mju'zɪʃn] Musiker/in

N
nasty ['nɑ:sti] gemein
nervous ['nɜ:vəs] nervös
nod [nɒd] nicken
notice ['nəʊtɪs] bemerken

O
obey [ə'beɪ] sich halten an, befolgen
offer ['ɒfə] Angebot
on [ɒn]: **You're on.** Du bist dran. Dein Auftritt.
one and only ['wʌnənd'əʊnli] einzigartig
one day ['wʌn'deɪ] eines Tages
onto ['ɒntu:] auf
opera ['ɒprə] Oper

P
pale [peɪl] blass
part [pɑ:t] Anteil
pat [pæt] leicht klopfen
peaches and cream ['pi:tʃɪzənd'kri:m] Pfirsiche und Sahne (hier etwa: Pfirsichhaut)
photographer [fə'tɒgrəfə] Fotograf/in
pick up ['pɪkʌp] aufheben
pineapple ['paɪnæpl] Ananas
pirouette [pɪrʊ'et] Pirouette
power ['paʊə] Leistung
powerfully ['paʊəfəli] kraftvoll, eindringlich
press [pres] drücken
promise ['prɒmɪs] **1.** versprechen; **2.** Versprechen
puberty ['pju:bəti] Pubertät
pure [pjʊə] rein, pur
purpose [pɜ:pəs]: **on purpose** absichtlich, mit Absicht
push [pʊʃ] schieben
put on [pʊt'ɒn] anziehen

R
rang [ræŋ] s.p. von **ring**
rap [ræp] rappen
reckon on something ['rekən] mit etwas rechnen
regular ['regjələ] normal
remember [rɪ'membə] daran denken
repeat [rɪ'pi:t] wiederholen
rest [rest] Rest
ring [rɪŋ] läuten; klingeln
ruin ['ru:ɪn] ruinieren, verderben
rule [ru:l] Regel

S
sang [sæŋ] s.p. von **sing**
second ['sekənd] Sekunde
secret ['si:krət] Geheimnis
serious ['sɪəriəs] ernst
shadow ['ʃædəʊ] Schatten
shine [ʃaɪn] scheinen, leuchten; glänzen
shoe [ʃu:] Schuh
shook [ʃʊk] s.p. von **shake**
shoulder ['ʃəʊldə] Schulter
shower ['ʃaʊə] Dusche
shut up [ʃʌt'ʌp] den Mund halten
size [saɪz] Größe
slim [slɪm] schlank
smell [smel] riechen
so: so that [səʊ'ðæt] damit; **So what!** ['səʊ'wɔt] Na und?
solidarity [sɒlɪ'dærəti] Solidarität
solve [sɒlv] lösen
sound [saʊnd] klingen
spell [spel] buchstabieren
stage [steɪdʒ] Bühne
stage fright ['steɪdʒfraɪt] Lampenfieber
stammer ['stæmə] stottern
stand [stænd] stehen
star [stɑ:] Stern
startled ['stɑ:tld] erschreckt
step [step] Schritt
stereo ['sterɪəʊ] Stereoanlage
stick [stɪk] Stöckchen, Stab
strength [streŋθ] Kraft
strong [strɒŋ] stark
stuck [stʌk] s.p. von **stick**
suntanned ['sʌntænd] sonnengebräunt, braungebrannt
sure [ʃʊə]: **he was sure of this** dessen war er sich sicher
surprise [sə'praɪz] Überraschung; **in surprise** überrascht
switch off [swɪtʃ'ɒf] abschalten, ausschalten

T
take [teɪk] bringen; **take a big step** einen großen Schritt tun; **take turns** [teɪk'tɜ:nz] sich abwechseln
technical ['teknɪkl] technisch
throat [θrəʊt] Kehle; Hals
tied back [taɪd'bæk] zurückgebunden
title ['taɪtl] Titel
ton [tʌn] Tonne
tough [tʌf] zäh; schwer, hart
towards [tə'wɔ:dz] auf ... zu, in Richtung
trial shoot ['traɪəlʃu:t] Probeaufnahmen
traitor ['treɪtə] Verräter/in
trousers ['traʊzəz] Hose
true [tru:]: **come true** wahr werden
trust [trʌst] vertrauen
tummy ['tʌmi] Bauch

U
unsure [ʌn'ʃʊə]: **they were unsure of themselves** sie waren unsicher

V
verse [vɜ:s] Strophe
voice [vɔɪs] Stimme

W
watch [wɔtʃ] Armbanduhr
wave (to) [weɪv] (zu)winken
weigh [weɪ] wiegen
welcome ['welkəm]: **Let's give a warm welcome to Luke.** Lasst uns Luke herzlich begrüßen.
while ['waɪl] Weile
whisper ['wɪspə] flüstern
whistle ['wɪsl] **1.** pfeifen; **2.** Pfeife
whizz [wɪz] zischen
whole [həʊl] ganz
wise [waɪz] weise, klug
worm [wɜ:m] Wurm
worst [wɜ:st] schlechteste/r/s, schlimmste/r/s
worth [wɜ:θ]: **it isn't worth it** es lohnt sich nicht
write down [raɪt'daʊn] aufschreiben
writing block ['raɪtɪŋblɒk] Schreibblock
wrong [rɒŋ]: **go wrong** schief gehen; **You're wrong.** Du hast / Sie haben Unrecht.